Hat on a Pond

Books by Dara Wier

Blood, Hook & Eye
The 8-Step Grapevine
All You Have in Common
The Book of Knowledge
Blue for the Plough
Our Master Plan
Voyages in English
Hat on a Pond

Hat on a Pond

Poems by

Dara Wier

Verse Press
Amherst, MA

Published by Verse Press

Library of Congress Cataloging-in-Publication Data
Wier, Dara, 1949-
Hat on a Pond : poems / by Dara Wier.— 1st ed.
    p. cm.
  ISBN 0-9703672-6-0 (pbk. : alk. paper)
  I. Title.
  PS3573.I357 H37 2001
  811'.54—dc2001
                                        2001006106

Printed in the United States of America

9 8 7 6 5 4 3 2 1

FIRST EDITION

ACKNOWLEDGMENTS: *American Letters & Commentary, American Literary Review, American Poetry Review, Both, Conduit, Crab Orchard Review, Crazy Horse, Denver Quarterly, Ducky, Fence, LIT, Margie, The Massachusetts Review, New Letters, Seattle Review, Slope, Verse, Virginia Quarterly Review, Volt, Willow Springs*

A selection of these poems was awarded the Jerome J. Shestack Poetry Prize by the Editors of American Poetry Review

for Jim

Table of Contents

"A small spool of number 50 white cotton thread, about half gone and half unwound. A cracked roseflowered china shaving mug, broken along the edge. A much worn, inchwide varnish brush stands in it. Also in the mug are eleven rusty nails, one blue composition button, one pearl headed pin (imitation), three dirty kitchen matches, a lump of toilet soap. A pink crescent celluloid comb: twenty-seven teeth, of which three are missing; sixteen imitation diamonds. A nailfile. A small bright mirror in a wire stand."

JAMES AGEE, *Let Us Now Praise Famous Men*

Balsam of Myrrh

Balsam of being here
With you and a thoughtful beetle,
With a sense of a wishful dime,
Who stood the sea on end and said
Go nap awhile in nigh egg room,
Get ye to some fish hatchery,
With your compass & passkey,
Your tin pitcher and bent cup,
Inside a cut a boy drew in his sleep
As he cut a slice of bread in his thumb,
By way of the several bridges a girl
Spends all night sweeping,
Red pears in pairs of ruby hands,
Oh, to be your sleeve, your shell,
Your lunar rover, your radial skin,
Your straw, your spacesuit, your neckline,
Your smoke working its way through a crack
In a skull, examining a breaking headline,
Ditchwater green handgrenades in pairs
Of identical hands, what did you do for
The twins and the sextuplets, is there nothing
You don't keep up your sleeve, you with all
The time in the world, bird with one wing.

Last Syllable of Recorded Time

Remember the clothcover, a scythe of red,
A blue membrane, green fingerprints, creases
Where creases need to be, where an eye can
Begin an education and twine, twine-binding
Keeping itself where it's wound, crossed, tied,
Deep inside a backroom's locker, our secret
Hiding place, lover, a room inside the water
Of a waterfall, behind our trick pilot's
Tailspin, inside a door between its keyhole
And doorknob, inside the second note in a
Boiling pot, where there's nothing left but
A drop of milk. One of those kind of places,
It involves a ritual & a speechless messenger,
Blinding light and a sleeptalking sphinx,
Black smoke condensed on a sheet of glass.
We know exactly what it feels like and we don't
Know what it is.

Awe of Everything

Do you know what's the unluckiest thing
In the world, a differential grasshopper
Said to me. I paused, I put down the
Diesel grinder I'd been trying to fix,
I turned off the stealth bomber, I faded
Away from the faded away pedals, I put up
Finely embroidered silk panels over the
Faces of the statues, I pulled the green
Vacillating amplifier into the hallway,
I swiveled seven of the chains and
Loosened the bolts in the balcony, I went
Into the barn to unlace the cattle and
Overturn the empty buckets, I put the
White flag on the mailbox, I cut the
Telephone wires, I fed the ducks better
Than I usually feed them, I adjusted the
Faucets so they'd drip a little, I waved
At old Mr. Wiley with his smokeless pipe
And his manpowered plough across the field,
I moved a claypot off of a narrow ledge,
I taped the key to the bulldozer to the
Roof of the canopy, I took the cup of
Auger bits away from the rabbit hutch,
I put a padlock on the children's playhouse,
I picked up a stick by the sideyard gate,
I broke it over my knee, I went to the well
To fill a stone pitcher with cool water,
I let the donkey & the goats go. I took
A ladder to the hayloft and took down a
Suitcase. I could see across the valley
Down to the river from up there.

To Keep Keep Away

Brainchild, little lotus-eater,
Your breath's as sweet as dew
On a nipple, fair featherfoil,
Where do you go when you're gone
So many years, mirage on the range,
What's that playing with your hammer,
Anvil & stirrup, changeling, ambivert,
What's that stirring in your hair,
Amnesiac, your skin went one way
And you went the other, what's that,
Brother smithereens, nobody's left
In the pesthouse, leave your flowers
At the gate, high priest on a blind horse,
Who covered the road with sheets of black ice?

Me & My Mantilla

Because I wasted a day in exchange
For something worthless I wanted punishment.
I started with a fairly important 20th century
Philosopher's earliest writings. He, who had
Profound plenty to say on just about every subject,
Said, talking women are possessed. Accidifying
Words, chain lightning, but not sufficient punish-
Ment for my crime. My mantilla, my two mantilla,
My white mantilla of raw silk, my black mantilla
Of blue shantung. I lay the black one over my
Latest snake in the grass, some air, some light
Can still get in and a snake in the grass stirring
Beneath black lace is a pretty thing. Too many,
Too many melismatic occasions, I think, was I sleep-
Walking in the skyways to miss that one, the one
With a mouth to be kissed, with arms & legs to
Consider. Out from under my mantilla my eyes fell
Over the airways stirring with the words for sorry.
For regret, for very, very, sorry, still not finding
Punishment enough to fit my crime. The day I wasted
Wasn't ever going to come around again, and wasn't
That slashing reproach enough?

Eye Lost in a Viewfinder

Eyes left behind on a riverbank, nose
Forgotten in orange blossoms, one hand
Still in bed, one putting down a mourning ring,
Another pushing back a twist of hair,
Feet still walking a moss path beside a canebrake,
A foot pulled out of a muddy workboot, an elbow
Lying forever over the back of a churchpew,
Mouth just opening over a nipple, wrists
Still floating over a water basin, open palm
Left on a fence post, an ear forgotten
Next to a keyhole, an eye stuck on a rifle's sight,
Fingers left in the flank fur of a half-cured pelt,
On an edge of a wicked green accordion pleat,
Near a locked diary with a key beside it, foot
Left a foot deep in riversand, feet forgotten
In party shoes, in a bucket of smoke, on a wooden
Plank over a flooded ditch, an ankle balanced
Forever on the edge of a table, forefinger &
Thumb left behind on a radio dial, ear unable
To leave a warm telephone receiver, eyes left
Dim in a room where someone's died,
Nose lost in a hurricane's eye,
Forgotten shoulder strap, face lost for good
In a silver compact mirror, face left behind
Blue curtain sheers, arms forgotten in sleeves
Of a suede jacket's satin lining, heel forgotten
In a bowl of dust, wrists hung on a hook with a
Coil of rope, ears forgotten halfway into a song,
Hand left halfway into opening a fish,
Fingers left working a sweatband back into place,
Teeth left on both sides of a collarbone, knees
Left in a melon field, neck left

Where a hand went too tight around it, neck lost
Where a mouth brought it back to life, eyes
Forgotten in flames inside a fireplace, hand
Misplaced on a clothespin, hand reluctant to leave
A cheekbone, hand hidden in a work glove, wrist
Forgotten on the handle of a sideblade, fingers
Left in a braid down the length of a back, some
Fingers forgotten in a bowl of rice.

Devilhorses

Sadie looked how someone in a cocktail
Dress feeding on a skunk looks.
Willie looked like a brain surgeon without
A plan.
Little Melvin looked cute in his surplus altar
Boy frock but he was a nasty kid, the kind of
Kid who does a lot of harm, silent as a hammer
Hammering air.
Papa Bill was teaching a bucket of shrimp to
Whistle and his older sister, Durable Claudia
Had already successfully taught armadillos how
To turn themselves into handbags.
Nearly everyone in the family was doing good.
Sister Sylvia had achieved some sort of synthesis
But she couldn't find the words to describe it.
Big Buck Harlow had his brains around a recipe
For marzipan. His always looked like figs &
Persimmons & fiddles.
Shirley used her nictitating membrane to give
Us the creeps and remind us who we were.
Henri & Joilee & Christian kept the goats out of
The icebox.
My job was to lie still as a stilletto in the
Grass, make myself as if invisible and wait for
The devilhorses to appear. A devilhorse is about
3 to 4 inches high. A devilhorse is black & red
And looks as if a tiny horse and its rider have
Been forged together into one highly stylized,
Modernized, predestined creature picking its way
Over the horizon, searching for the face of a
Child, child with nothing to fear.

Sea Foam

Tomorrow is today's perfect thought.
Saffron threaded through the central heating
System known as marrow.
God the Father's perfect thought they say
Turns out to be his son and later on our savior.
They say these jokers first good long gander,
Instantaneous glances one upon the other, arrives
With so much force what registers upon them is the
Holy Ghost, who later on will wield a tongue of fire,
And later on will bless us.
Tomorrow's perfect thought just begins to divide
Somewhere deep inside a drop of rain just now
Beginning to condense inside a cloud in someone's
Mind. The almighty love triangle mentioned above
Has gone on to greater things. Meanwhile it will
Have become apparent to my owner that it is high time
To take me down from my shelf and put me to good use.
But, alas, first I will need to be tuned.

A Ghost's List of Alarming Notes
After a Drizzling Rain

Pockets of rats in money alley,
Ball of worms pretending it's a brain,
Opalish with poplars in the mountains,
Rarely entered, it happens everywhere along the palms,
Sometimes everything looks like that,
Dopey song & dance situations,
Something was thwarting with the fishes,
The nose appeared to be especially suspicious,
A sound of a bus station permeated,
Something about a solar system altered a birdbath,
It was near where a field leading up to a mountain had been,
There were two sets of landing gear on the porch,
The one on the left held something in its mouth,
They had taken their whiskers off,
For a few seconds very exciting key & button conversation,
They were napping with their heads down on the conversion
    tables,
Original sin popped in, felt sadly neglected,
A thermostat peed on the rug,
There was part of a story sticking out from behind the 7th
One's ear,
Where guilt was was as confusing as oil over water,
The colors came from the world where chemical storage tanks
Burned,
There were too many different kinds of temperature,
Always something in or after or behind or over,
Never anywhere for armbands,
Not one of them went anywhere without their bones,
A light rain dappled their soulpaper.

Green Veil Against the Sun

Mother's on fire a small child says
Sweetly to an ant. Dad's moonstruck
A small child says sweetly to a bee,
All up in smoke. Everyone was kissing
The glass on both sides of the windows
Of a passing train.

An Error Lurks in Such a Certainty

An eraser barks in South Carolina.
A bag of tickets blows into Nova Scotia.
A bottle of water circumnavigates the Maritimes.
A pencil sharpener ascends Mt. Everest.
A bus believes it is a thumbtack.
A baby turns itself inside out and nobody notices.
A pigeon assumes it has found all the answers.
Two doorways fall in love.
A broken-hearted drummer is confronted by a wind-
Shield wiper.
A train curls up on a couch cushion and dreams
It is stalking a squirrel.
A stick of butter dreams it is carrying a load of
Coal across the Badlands, in moonlight, on Monday.
A windmill gives birth to sixteen umbrellas.
A table fan reverses the course of a river.
A drill bit examines its conscience.
A plate of ribs invents perpetual motion.
A fishing pole replaces the Defense Department.
A piece of toast travels to Saturn.
A glove remarks on the beauty of sidewalks.
A cymbal explores the depths of an ocean.
A safety pin kisses a wolverine.
Some kneebritches send out a round of apologies.
A crease saves the eyewitness from anthrax.
In the Earth's core a school of sunfish braid
Fine lariats for lovers of this world.

Reflection on a Shopwindow Filled with Mirrors

I wouldn't have known if I hadn't looked,
Wouldn't have paid attention to a pay phone,
Wouldn't have picked up its receiver.
Sweet one, a calm voice said, take hold
Of one end of a rope.
I wore a cloche with an arrow attached.
I might have bought one orange and left it at that.
I got off one stop sooner to make the walk longer.
Some coils of circuit binding shoved me hither.
I found a bar code pressed into my forearm.
I longed for a little reverse osmosis to set in.
A streetcar full of roses passed through my breasts,
A police officer and his horse in the vicinity of my heart,
A woman in a black raincoat helping a blind white dog cross
The street, satchels, extra lapels, book of matches.
A revolving door revolved no more.
I could have left the watch where I'd found it,
Pulled out a thread and forgotten all about it,
Kept my lips sealed, saved someone the bother.
If I hadn't heard I wouldn't have listened,
Wouldn't have thought about a guitar player's fingers,
Wouldn't have put my hand in his side,
I might have ignored the glove and the broken yardstick,
Might have missed someone I love open a mailbox,
Have been elsewhere when a bucket of bones fell off a roof.
Flocks of birds & falling leaves have been having their way
With my subatomic particles. Zaffer blue neon and a felon
Wind, fellow travelers.

Endless Afternoons in a Spring Ice Storm on Mountain Roads in the Poconos

We followed a set of watery tire tracks through a series
Of dusty trails. We stayed nearby one another, we stuck
Next to the guard rails. Hoarfrost made an impression on
Us.

We followed the wet tire tracks along a dusty road until
We came to a railway crossing with lights flashing and
A bell ringing with no train coming. But we heard the horn's
Blast.

But we never saw it coming. On & off we talked about boxing
And who might be the next world featherweight champion,
Maybe the one with the eyes of an Egyptian prince, handsome
Muslim.

We went on in sleet and rain and fog up to where trees grew
Shorter by the hour and deer alongside the road were always
Dead and sometimes deader than we remembered deer could
Ever be.

We went up where charcoal stumps interrupted freezing pools
In places water froze. If there were views or vistas they
Were rumors clouds and mist poured over like tangled thoughts
Of lovers.

Off & on we talked about the lengths we go to pretend we're
Immortal and who might be the first of our kind to stumble
Upon one of the thousands of misplaced philosopher's stones
Very soon.

We followed where the road went between strafed granite walls
Weeping ice blue water with our eyes closed, with our thoughts
On cruise control, where the road rose and rose and we fell
In a cloud.

We went with the cloud without leaving the road as far as we
Could. We leaned closer to one another as the road went by.
We passed a doe & fawn eating by the side of the road where
Snow wasn't.

Off & on we talked about what happens when we love someone
Who doesn't love us. We figured in what happens to friends
When they go their separate ways. Soon we were mist, we were
Numb.

Feral Boy

The feral boy showed up everywhere
We went that day. While we waited
For the woman who owns the tobacco
Shop to explain to her son why he's
Not allowed to sell tobacco products,
Too young, the feral boy slipped behind
Our backs and up & down the aisles of
Every kind of magazine in the world and
Was gone. When we talked with the men
In the music store about a sound that makes
You feel as if the music is happily heading
In one direction while the musician is always
Dragging it back in some other direction, the
Feral boy sobbed a muffled whoa, and shuffled
Behind us to the back of the shop, up & down
The aisles of every kind of music and was gone.
When we stood on the sidewalk next to a burned
Wall saying, Looking for a Good Home for a
Goldfish, the feral boy tiptoed by, turned a
Corner into a single-file alleyway and was gone.
When we spoke with the jeweler over where and
In what sort of letters we'd have the baby's
Name etched on her silvercup, the feral boy
Hovered near around us around and around every kind
Of precious gem and metal in the world, looked
Past our shoulders, took note of the baby's
Name and was gone. Later in the sandwich shop
While we talked with a neighbor about a recent trip
he'd made down Memory Lane, the feral boy
Stirred behind our backs and stopped briefly
To look into our hearts and was gone.

Novelization

One transaction involved apple pies,
& a man slouched down in a black chair
Waiting for his wife and her lover to appear.
Once it had to do with too much lime juice.
One of them cheated in a friendly poker game.
The man had strong feelings about a dishcloth.
A woodstove controlled half of every day.
She told me who she really was.
He threw a hammer at his dog.
He peed around the perimeters of his garden.
He threw a television from a second-story window.
He slipped on a sidewalk & cracked his skull.
He mixed her a Manhattan.
She said she'd seen him on television.
They nearly came to blows at the mention of a name.
She slipped on a wet plank walk and broke an ankle.
Once it involved visiting the sick.
Once it had to do with housekeeping.
A stolen chicken figured into part of it.
A handprint bloodprint never washed out of a green silk shirt.
She carried a basket when they shopped for Sunday suppers.
One of them could recite a long poem about a fiddler.
Once he wanted to leave without paying a bill.
One day he shaved off his beard.
She'd never worn make-up before.
A tumbleweed blew through the room right on time.
Once it involved an emerald green chemise & a fuzzy pink
    sweater.
Twice a masseuse had something to do with it.
Often a playhouse came into play.
Indigo buntings almost changed everything.
It was dotted with keys, doorknobs, a ringing telephone,

Footsteps & breathing.

A trout, a bass, sac au lait and a contact lens participated.

Every kind of weather always had a hand in it.

Official holidays could be counted part of it.

She could be broken down with flowers, stopped short with a

Center of a poppy, brought to her knees near sweet olive.

Cockroaches flew in and out of it.

She didn't always know what fingers were for.

It was nicked everywhere with hailstones & sleet.

She was afraid of housefuls of napping grown-ups.

There had been two terribly long train rides.

It was mixed up with a horse with a Roman nose.

Once something happened with ice in a glass.

A towtruck, a rockslide, a featherduster, a dove

& a duck.

Once a man passed out on a country road needed to be

Included.

She thought something light-flecked could solve everything.

A camel led a caravan along a canal one evening.

Headphones, a canvas bag, a palm-size whetstone

Of blue crabs had been reckoned with.

A torn blouse.

He stretched out on the hearth & tried to go to sleep.

He walked like a lynx on its hindfeet.

He did his best work in a smuggling act.

Sometimes sheets of glass were indicated.

Once the San Antonio river was in the background.

A house alarm that wouldn't shut off was a fluke.

In the corner of a blanket someone's initials had been sewn.

Once a farmer offered them peaches for lunch.

Volcanic dust couldn't apologize.

Anti-twilight arches were always there.

A face marked with candleblack couldn't explain.

Illumined with the Light of Fitfully Burning Censers

Intelligent voice of a suburban housewife,
Present & accounted for, sir.
Really got a good deal on those filters,
On that service, on these curtains, really
Got a good parking place, good appointment
With the orthodontist, with the guidance
Counselor, really did well with the raffle
Tickets, with the ceviche and raisin salad,
Got a really good parking place, finished
That coffee off in a hurry, got a really
Good deal with that housekeeper, her husband
Wants to do yardwork as well, got a really
Good deal with the babysitter her mother's
A seamstress on the side. On the side of
What, did not ask. Got a really good deal
On napkins, felt good about their color, got
An okay parking place, did pretty well with
The birdseed, got a great deal on the flag-
Stone, really found a decent way to get out
Of the committee work, wrote seven thank-
You notes, sent flowers quite easily, got
A really good parking place, made an excel-
Lent Cobb salad, found a shortcut to the
Fishmarket, remembered the fishmonger's name,
Remembered to pick up the dry cleaning, to
Pass by the wine shop, got an okay parking place,
Checked into fall schedules, got a perfect
Appointment with the accountant, made real
Headway with the holiday schedule, found the
Perfect gift for my sister, remembered to
Check at the postoffice for the missing
Delivery, noticed the new postal rates, looked

At the wanted posters, went to the bank, spoke
With the teller about foreign currency, saw
Myself on a telemonitor, looked up a recipe
For buffalo, got a lousy parking space, felt
Really good about everything that got done
Today, picked up a magazine, said no to a
Solicitor, placed an order, checked on the
Buffalo, read a book by, dreamed
He was my wife.

Fugue Pirogue on Bayou St. John

Reviviscence, what we call
Our destination, what we sew
Inside our hems, what we hew
With our oars into heavy waters,
With our poles exploring
Marshbeds, with chenier
To bump into.
Baby, baby, baby,
How our wake reaches
Back to the blue banks,
How our whimpers nose
Their way home,
How our fingers forget
What they've touched.
Winds ticking through liveoak,
Through our hair lifting off
Our foreheads, our headlights
Pretending to be eyes,
Our terror-blinded, water-
Soaked wishes, what we say
To them when they die.

Precious Celestial Membrane

I'd fallen off my tricycle
And you said, good, do it again.
My echo chamber was filling with
Pure cane syrup, with eruptions
Of June bugs. I'd stared for 7
Hours straight at the hairs on a
Cricket's head. I think my head
Had a hole drilled in it. Slowly
It had been filled with starch.
A cranky old laundress was firing
Up her irons and thinking about
Pleats. Hyperspectrality washed
Over us and we washed over it.
You knew how much I liked to watch
Dusk creep around the planet.
You remembered how I'd sit for hours
On the riverbank waiting for something
To happen. You saw me standing behind
A fan listening to soundwaves break.
When I saw an ant crawling on your cuff
I touched my wrist, experts of the
Figure eight, ants of the expanding
Universe, eyeteeth of the reknowned
Eternal life.

Turtles all the Way Down

Someone took the thought, applied
Mascara to it and drew circles around
It with charcoal, ink & kohl.
It would look good with that other thought,
The one circumambulating beneath the pines
Pretending it's a dove. Whole town nippled
With steeples, whole sun hidden behind a
Thumbprint, hereby I offer my services to
You, let me be your ritual object.
A man named Samuel Clemens has provided me
With some of the means by which to approach
Descending. These are our words:
I will descend slowly, mine, and cautiously
And timorously, his, and piously and solemnly,
His, which will cause me to feel dreamy and,
Mine, creepy and crawly and scary and, his,
Frozen and wobbling, mine, and dismal and
Repentant, ours, and I will continue descending
Turtle by turtle, careful not to poke one
In the eye or step too firmly on their flexible
Necks. If I may suggest a tentative conjecture
Knowing full well the limits of my experience,
Eventually I will come to a turtle which is
Standing on the invincible ultimate mirror,
It will call me "fallen angel" and I will
Surrender "spitfire."

Immolation of the Blue Inscriptions

Black canal half & half hyacinths &
Inkluster slow water, influx almighty
With mosquito hawks, the blue kind
Rotating through green ones speeding
Like mad over orange gold flame models,
They want something politically activated,
They want justice, they want money,
Park benches, a little boat, a teaspoon
Of real cream, hyacinths half unfurled
Half hypnotizing kingfishers and cattails,
They want to participate in the human genome
Project, to seek equality in the laundry,
They want a good pair of shoes & a decent meal.
They want an armadillo almighty influx among
The inane assemblies, they want a donkey &
A tame raccoon, a few of them want to crush
The competition though they say so ever-so
Gently, blue ones rotating like mad over
Gold samples, they want a big red umbrella,
A blooming field of mustard & lavender,
Coal trains under blue skies flying over red rails,
A genius of a doctor with a heart of uranium,
Saint of a lawyer with no hidden agenda,
They want to be motivated by peach pits &
Grass clippings, an abandoned hat factory,
A lost metal detector, slow water canal
Nudging up under cathedrals of cypress-stopping
Oil rig installations, lesser cranes & great
Ibis figuring out price controls, they want
Good schools for their happy offspring,
Protection from West Nile virus, they want
A bowl of cold ripe figs, flagtips of bulrush,

They want to whisper to air traffic control
Operators, they want to donate their eyes
To science, they dream of comparing notes with
The great Baseline Array, when they fly in
Reverse they switch a day back several notches,
They make arrangements to supply more zeroes,
They spend their nights mending family feuds
And committing weavework in yon matrix.

Day After a Funeral

Orange blossoms smell like the insides
Of a drop of orange flesh. Orange blossoms
Vie with gardenias, with lemongrass teas,
With the empty insides of a cocktail purse
Opened one evening at the beginning of the
20th century and never opened since. Paths
Smoothed over by footsteps carrying a boy
In search of a fox, a girl carrying a box
She's painted with black roses, footsteps
Under a widow unlocking her side door, switching
Off her porchlight, under a boy carrying his
First casket, under an undertaker eating a sandwich,
Under a girl reading a book and rocking a baby,
Under a dog racing after the scent of its master.

Stucco'd with Quadrupeds and Birds All Over

Lacquered with roses, with rich black dirt,
Bled blue with water striders and better for it,
Imprisoned with blind justice and desire,
With shrill whistles and fading histories,
Inched into by parts of speech, handled by tides,
Polished with handling, glanced with watchsprings,
And bootheels, rocked with glass splinters,
With icedarts, proofread by priests of the order
Of the surfaces of water, by pigeons collecting
Evidence at the scene of a crime, plundered
With tastebuds, with fingerprints, smothered
With telephone numbers, with tales of woe,
Battered with questions without good answers,
Wreathed with souppots and chance, hammered
With never again, too late, not in this lifetime,
Wagered with a couple of strands of hair,
A collar, a twist of fate, a row of simple buttons.

Fear of Psychic Surgery

His mother said she wished she'd never been born
So that he'd never been born so that now she would not
Have to kill herself. He says all this with a smile
Nodding as he tells us that his mother's still alive
And he's still doing what it was caused her to say
Such things to begin with. He says if he went looking
For an excuse to stop all he'd need to do is turn over
A rock. The rocker he's sitting in while he's talking
Creaks so hard all of us are afraid it's about to break
So he stands up to investigate and while it certainly
Is wobbly and one can see where it's been repeatedly
Repaired it doesn't appear he shouldn't sit back down
And continue with his story. He never mentions a
Father or anyone else in his family. He says he's
Been fleeing his hometown since the minute he was born,
If he hadn't gotten away he'd have done himself in.
Like mother, like son, one of us lamely jokes to which
He replies, yes, all the time we are extremely disinclined
Suicides. At which point one of us rears his head back
So hard it bounces off its nail and falls without breaking
At our feet. It's fine so we put it back where it belongs
And wait for him to get back to his story, but he wants
To think about the picture which is a drawing in charcoal
Of a pear and an apple overlapping without canceling one
Another out, a simple optical trick, a cool illusion,
He says, something that isn't that way and couldn't be
Otherwise. He says who needs excuses anyway. One of us
Agrees and accompanies assent with a somewhat exaggerated
Arm-length sweeping gesture. Across the room a white
Hyacinth tips out of its bowl onto the table. One of us
Is a witch's daughter but nobody tells him this.
Suddenly he asked for his coat. Suddenly we all stood up.

Mission Statement of the Chamber of Commerce

Once in awhile they found one another trying
On shoes.
Sometimes they could be found percolating on
Plumtree Road.
There had been no good explanation for the pyramids
Of dust.
Most often during the horse exchange the horses
Never changed.
Remind us not to get started on the list of bad
Signs.
Later that evening they were tired after rolling their
Eyes and winking at the same time.
We extracted a promise there'd be no more harping.
They said it was okay to do push-ups in pedalpushers.
After all of the edges had returned to their corners
And did stupefying stunts it resulted in what could
Be looked upon as just another instance of a quasi-
Momentary-stay-against-confusion
Most likely drowsy with nightlife.
They bottled the smell of starch steaming up from
A collar on a cotton blouse.
Usually the most difficult ones had the softest hearts.
See the appendix for more.
It didn't help to be thinking a little too far ahead
Of oneself.
It could induce paralysis, or accelerated untethering.
It occasionally caused them to find themselves inside
Undivided attention.
They found themselves in an inventory (no one could see
The beginning of.)
It didn't help to go flipping back & forth between enter-
Tain and console as if these were alternating currents.

But sometimes it did.
All of the first words were *I want an echo*.
The one who said school is not cute was suffering from
Incurable iridescence.
Much of what happened went on inside mammals.
We needed to indicate that it would make sense to stop
Interfering with the kittens
Frankincense is a fact that explains clearcut forgetfulness.
Now & then there were eyes all over their heads
During daydreams when grasshoppers played interludes
On their glass violins.

The Appendix

The ones with the softest hearts divide
Their time between nearly dead and almost alive.
One may have a soft heart and not be a soft touch.
One with a soft heart may often be referred to as
No slouch, often as not.
It is possible to locate a soft heart in a stiff dick.
I mean, it is possible to locate a soft heart in a starched shirt.
Soft hearts are always losing their soulmates.
It is not unusual for a soft heart to be a hard case.
A couple of soft hearts is called complaint department.
A dozen soft hearts is known as a combat zone.
Soft hearts stay away from where angels fear to tread.
A soft heart is rarely the mastermind of a minefield.
The most desirable soft hearts are filled with goosedown.
An injured soft heart must be taken to a forest.
It must not be seen by a dentist.
It should be repaired rather than recycled or incinerated.
Eventually a tinker will pass by who will know what to do.
You will know him by his long eared patient pack animal
With big liquid eyes.
It is important not to forget that sometimes a bad egg
Has managed to make itself look like a soft heart.
In this event one should not be too hasty with the poison
Dart. Inside a bad egg is sometimes some kind of heart
Involved in some sort of transition. Nevertheless.
A soft heart is not an insect or an anecdote.
Evidence of interactions among soft hearts and parasites
And predators can be found in the next appendix.
Caution: soft hearts are extremely shy and do not wish
To be seen; for this reason upon encountering one it may
Put on a great show that it is indeed its very opposite;
This is quite natural and should be tolerated without

Comment, remark or interference.
In some circumstances it is good luck to touch a soft heart.
In the next section we will pay some attention to their
Geographical range.

Contrast of Blues with an Element of Orange
in the Golden Bronze of Corn

At this time we still farmed
And hadn't yet finished

With our eyes.
It would be a while

Before we stopped wearing shoes.
Soul exchanges

Operated underground
Without regulation.

Have you ever been blind-folded
Without wanting to be seen?

We'd lived through nine utopia
And it showed.

We were promised
It would be the last time

We'd be turned inside out
Or reversed.

Some looked all right in silhouette,
Even outlined in orange.

There were still brides
And grooms of many different kinds.

A kiss was still
A kiss at this time.

Instances of Wasted Ingenuity

Falling off a triangle.
Putting two fighting fish in one bowl.
Talking yourself into a headcold.
Falling off a rectangle.
Putting insects in ice cubes.
Talking yourself out of doorways.
Falling off a parallelogram.
Talking into a microphone.
Falling off a footstool.
Putting earplugs in acorns.
Looking into a teacup for trouble.
Talking yourself out of breathing.
Taking a nap on a drum set.
Eating a peach with an air filter.
Wearing a dress made of hand grenades.
Talking a mudslide back up a mountain.
Lighting a camp fire in a taxi stand.
Launching a boat on a horse trail.
Hiking in a elevator.
Falling into an envelope.
Discussing smuggling with customs officers.
Taking a cat to a dog show.
Falling in love with a toothache,
Questioning your thumbprint.
Looking for milk in a gas tank.
Kissing hydraulic acid.
Blindfolding a parking meter.
Falling over a water tower.
Reasoning with a baby.

Cleanliness, etc.

We're clean. That's a start.
What was it like moving steadily in the tracks
Of the human carwash? With crystal chandeliers
Lighting our path? Bellowing our fate.
What of the nearly destitute immigrants
Horsewhipped into working the detail line.
They looked at us with alarm. We had signs pinned
On our breasts: we are going to a funeral.
And that made everyone wary of us and caused them
All to bow a little in our direction as though
Towards their hard-earned suppers. Across the
Roadway their suppers waited on ice in the bed
Of a truck. They'd have a choice between roasted
Or stewed raccoon or deep fried snake. One of them
Made a big deal over wiping the last drop of water
From our rearview mirror. I wept.

Aerosol Prayer

I don't know what goes on.
Stuff with blood and wine, crosses, clouds
And roses, maybe cheese and sacred vessels.
Down the road I bumble with my load of things
For sale. Thimbles of dust I spend my time
Collecting from scores of sacred wells. Dust
For love, dust for money, dust for health, dust
To uncork the unborn, dust to plot revenge, dust
For animals, dust for friends. I have envelopes full
Of volcanic ash for many are those who find volcanoes
Irresistible. I have bottles and vials of waters
From the headwaters of all the rivers in the world,
And waters as well from the many springs opened by
The holiest of hands. I have an especially fine
Collection of tears—the usual suspects, drippings
From statues and portraits of saints, and my collection
Includes the rare tears of heads of state and money
Managers and the one tear ever shed by the man who
Invented the focus group. My treasures include first
Tears and last tears and tears that come out of nowhere
And fear. I somehow got the teardrop of a snake.
I have a wide-variety of tears shed in the darkest
Hours of those orphaned days known as over and done
With.

Election Night Blues

We've been allocated 27 events-per-unit,
Three of which may be considered major.
Check your vibration meters at the door.
Strictly black-tie for the bodyguards.
There will be a trading steward assigned
To each segment.
There will be a sequence of light artillery
Engagements before the scripture shredding.
You are encouraged to wear nothing
A sizable abyss will be proved on the terrace
And numerous less bulky ones will be scattered
In strategic locations. Use them wisely.
Enthusiasm will be rigorously curtailed.
Voluntary muscle inspectors will circulate or
Rotate or cycle or scatter or disperse or
Percolate or cruise or restrain or for that
Matter do whatever necessary.
Double-edged stuff should be kept to a minimum.
You'll be provided with bits of conversation
In ten words or less on fewer than one occasion.
A light fare will be sub-bland.
The band will keep the balls, cellars, crawlspaces,
Attics and walls free from animal and insect life.
There will be one degree of difference in room
Temperature at some point in the proceedings.
This is necessary in order to complete adjustments
On the strain gauges. No remarks needed.
Anyone found to be ambivalent will be asked to leave.
Different passwords are required for each of the cells.
If you have forgotten your password that is only natural

And you should drop your hands in your lap for a while.
You may stare into an abyss for as long as you like.
You are allowed to ask fellow party members for assistance.
Should one party member push another party member over the
Edge, she or he may not discuss it, not at this time.
Perhaps in the future, the very near future,
When we have identified the frontiers.

Nature

Housewrens had built a shabby nest
In an upper eave's broken gutter,
A wrong place, a poor chance we saw
As we walked by into crooked windgusts
Rising before most of the nest fell
At our feet, we had been lamenting
The loss of a friend to hard-earned
Brutal lunacy, we'd been lamenting
Our useless love and understanding,
As if love were a cart & understanding
A cordial donkey, and the wrens' nest
We saw was mixed media, dry wheat grass,
A strip of frayed red cotton, green
Fishing line, half of a half of a pair
Of blue wool mittens, a knotted coil
Of twisted cassette ribbon, some gray
Stripped cotton fluff and one of us
Had just said it's no use and stooped
To pick up an uncracked egg we saw
Was barely pulsing, a haggard face,
A wrong chance, all-knowing wind.

An Early Afternoon in Cummington, Massachusetts

It was like floating down a hallway
Of sleeping bees, one's very atomic cellwork
Felt especially suspended. A breeze blew us
Along the sleepy town's main drag, a good-
Looking dog greeted us with his hydro-electric
Panting. Oh my God, look, there's Stan Koehler
Standing in line to get into the church.
And Herman, with his cap and backpack on,
Walking on the sidewalk toward the church.
Lynette & Matthew and Christy come up, long out
Of breath, hoping to get into the church.
There's Ellen cruising for a parking place,
She's most certainly headed for the church.
Whole town filled with out-of-towners on a bee-
Line, shifting and shuffling up to the church.
You'd think they were after a free lunch or
Had heard the preacher possessed a tongue of
Fire & gold. Someone calls out from the church
Steps: Standing Room Only and it's hot as hell.
The line doesn't thin at all, it keeps getting
Longer. Gerald rushes up and asks if we've seen
His father-in-law and we say yes, he's already
In. Gerald cuts past everyone in line & goes
Straight into the church. The place could be
Filled with people we know. Maybe Christian's
Inside, with Alix and Mike, maybe James is
In there with Jack & Nicky on his knees.
Anyone could be in there by now, it's one of
Those places that never fills up, it seems.
For the second time today we walk past the
Ripped sheet of plywood with an arrow spray-painted
On its face. People can't get enough of that

Stuff, someone with flame-throwers in his eyes
Yells at us as he mounts his blazing blind horse.

Inside Job

We were stuck inside our job
And it was stuck inside a whale
And it was stuck inside an ocean
And it was stuck between East & West Timor
And it was stuck inside a timewarp
And it was stuck inside an airplane's landing
Gear and it was stuck inside a magazine rack
And it was stuck to a washing machine and it was
Stuck to a gluegun and it was stuck inside
A hobby shop and it was stuck between a buffalo
Farm and a veterinarian's office and they stood
Side by side next to a golf course and it stood
Out from the asphalt and megalomanic superstore
With not a single window in it and it was stuck
Without a soul and it was crying all night long
For someone to smash it back into its original
Parts and let it be sand, rock, stone, water &
Whatever petrochemicals, blueprints, pencil
Shavings, big, wide, alluvial plain with a pretty
Geeky kid running back & forth all over it
Pretending he rules the world.

Wishing There Were Some Better Ways of Explaining Ourselves to Birds

It's one o'clock in the ocean,
Nine in the morning on the nose of a mole,
Workday just beginning for carpenter ants,
Pencilsticks on holiday on a coral reef,
Sacred day for pants pockets, for handkerchiefs,
Anniversary of the invention of revolving doors,
Half-dreams that leave an impression walking
Through walls. It strikes me as strange when
Questions about birds have to do with whether
We can understand them. Sometimes a bird will
Look at me as if it has just read my mind or
As if it's wondering if I'll ever catch on.
Birds who've died crashing into glass walls
Come back to life as monks or nuns and every
Now & then as heavyweight championship boxers.
Does it snow where you are? Can you fry eggs?
Aren't our eyes strange, the way they stay open,
Then stay closed. Where did skinks get their
Bad reputations? When they're young their
Ornate blue and black markings make them easy
Pickings, then the ones who're left gradually
Turn brown as fine garden dust. It's one o'
Clock in the ocean. A slightly scarlet bullet
Races through a snowbank and lands on a sheet
Of black ice. A bird on its way to work notices,
Pauses, picks it up. What's happening on the
Golden spike, who's touched it today?

The Great Divide

He's yours but I would put him high over
The Great Plains leaning hard against a window
Looking down from a few seats behind a prop's
Right wingspan. He belongs to you but I would
Have him watching a road cross several rivers
And veer off into farmland, into fall's display
Of green diluting into gold, browns, beige and
Gray. I would have him follow a road into
Foothills along switchbacks to disappear in
Trees going up a mountain's eastside and reappear
As it leaves the treeline behind and crosses
The Great Divide. A stewardess would offer him
A highball and a filtered cigarette and he would
Thank her and settle back into watching
Snowfields and in one of these he'd see a herd
Of elk and in another one nothing. He belongs
To you but I'd watch him lean nearly clean through
The window to follow a car he can see racing
Over a narrow bridge and that's when he'd remember
His father who chose never to learn to drive
Because he believed if he did he'd kill someone,
Because his father had done just that and was
On record in a recordbook high somewhere up in
The Alps as the first man to kill another human
Being with a car. He's yours and if I were you
I'd give him a name, a family and a home.
I'd have him land near one of the big cities on
The West Coast and catch a train to a trolley line
And ride down to a port and sit on a bench
In front of where a small white fishing boat is
Docked. He'd tell a stranger sitting with him,
By his rightside, he'd come to wait for his father.
Then he would close his eyes.

Twisted, Fucked-Up, Poor Excuse

They were entertaining a serious argument
Concerning what they believed to be the dis-
Integration of the personal pronoun I as a
Viable sign for the self. A herd of mad
Bull elephants could be heard approaching
The city limits. Obviously they had all the
Time in the world. Rust was blossoming on
Them and they didn't notice it, but it was
Fascinating anyway. A boulder big as the
State of Texas was about to fall on the side-
Walk where they were talking but they were
In the midst of dismissing that curiously dis-
Integrating ironic lyrical I. A 9.5 on the
Richter scale earthquake was just getting
Started but they were stomping their feet
Saying I, I, I, and didn't really notice it.
Barbed wire clarity, one of them moaned,
Never self-celebratory, one of them sighed.
I was on my way to visit a good friend's
Grave, to visit a fox, box turtle and a
String of buttons. But what really stung
Was how during all of their mind-bending
Ratiocinations and obsessed self-consultation
They never once mentioned "me."

Boy in the Air

His grunting amazing as he uses it
Almost it seems to finish the job
He's started, jumping, jumping,
Springing from trampoline bed into
Thin air where while he's in it
Unattached anymore speechless, in
Contact once again with an endless
Summer morning, before his parents
Split, when he was just a boy, with
Nothing to lose, he bounces on his
Knees and up onto his feet, he slams
Down harder every time and winds up
Higher than he's ever been, executes
A slightly wobbly flip and then he's
Back at it, on his butt, on his knees,
On his feet, flipping, grunting, it's
Late on a winter afternoon, he's doing
All this in the dark, in the cold.
He doesn't think anyone's watching.

Hot Pursuit of the Unapproachable

I'll not try to nail in a screw with an icepick.
I'll not try to stitch an open wound with a fiddler's
Stick. I'll not try to write a prayer on a river
With flaming red lipstick, not try to find my way
Across the valley at night in a blizzard with a match-
Stick, try not to comb my hair with a walkingstick,
Not give directions with a crooked stick, not put
Out a fire with two sticks, not keep a promise with
A broken stick. I won't ask the catbird to think
About nightingales. I won't complain to an ant that
It is so very small. I won't ask mourning doves
To change their tune, to be less skitterish.
I won't sing within earshot of anyone. I won't take
Up tightrope walking. I won't ask the dead to stop
Talking, to let me borrow their brooms. I won't say
To a scorpion you'd look better in cufflinks, or ask
a tarantula to get a buzzcut. I won't ask the snake
What it overheard last week. I won't remind Chicago
What it was in the backtime or call Connecticut a
Corridor. I won't go into a bookstore and ask for a
Backhoe, or try to parallel park on an altar, or ask
For a splash of tears in my whiskey. I won't ask a
Zebra to blend in with baroque wallpaper or a great
Bengali tiger to lend its paws to a lawyer. I won't
Ask last year how it feels about tomorrow, or try to
Convince an oyster it has unlimited options, or talk
My pillow into believing what lies on it every night
Is a little less than the holy of holies.

Catalpa's Majesty

My love is a true catalpa parabola, latter-day
Catalpa sable, urban catalpa altar saucer, very
Very long catalpa arms, innocent catalpa eyes,
Ceaseless catalpa incunabula, endless numbers
Of petals catalpa lightning pitches over a continuous
Catalpa field, petals inscribed catalpa purple,
Electric animal sexual catalpa longing, blue,
Hydraulic catalpa memorization device, yellow,
Finger-print catalpa powder, white, catalpa emotion
Cyclotron, green catalpa windowframe reduction
Cluster, hand-drawn catalpa simple green, cut-
Catalpa-out-shaped catalpa hearts in some sort
Of baby catalpa's lovesick catalpa dream, a true
Catalpa godleash pictogram project, a catalpa
Talk into the catalpa light of day every green
Catalpa continuous shift, everyday catalpa zone
Broadcast, a catalpa encoded catalpa yearning
Counterplot, catalpa rain, catalpa no ceiling
Catalpa visibility snowball effect, ceaseless
Says my catalpa darling, ceaseless as a sea of
Catalpa hearts, for the time being, ceaseless
As leaves.

Soul Migration

Down in a shallow pasture off Station Road
In a pre-evaporated afternoon
A redemptive scattering of bubbling clouds
Shallow quicksilver heat mirages
Pasture where blue fescue & chicory blue
Off and dusted with evening primrose pollen
Station to station pick-up and delivery
Road less a road more a remote restoration
A second chance for shoelaces & shaving brushes
Small explosive devices of near resort
Herd instinct de-activated for now
Maybe forever will be arriving on time
Nine seconds late is just late enough
Head for the skyblue watering hole
Of who knew who more will be known later
Horses can help out in most transactions
Has the slack been adjusted
Been part way to glory and back again
Blindfolded in a pasture off Station Road

More Than We Knew What To Do With

Our streets filled with combines this fine
September afternoon, full moon inflated last
Evening. I went up with an air gauge to get
A reading. Poor moon, always under so much
Pressure. I looked down, a wisp of smoke
I saw rise from my true love's chimney.
After which inning do the stretching demonstrations
Begin? We played in the water tank all last night,
Displacing enough water to drown a whale, which is
Not something anyone of us could stand to see go on,
Yet we had to admit not a one of us would know how
To stop it. And it would be so pointless.
Then you said, let's talk about points.
Larry said the point would be to take care of someone
Nobody cared for. The baby's head had been pointy
For longer than anyone cared to admit. It's not
Pointy now but when it was it made a deep impression.
Lorraine said that's my point.
Gerard said he'd always pictured points in broad daylight
Though he knew he shouldn't be so pollyannaish.
Then he mentioned pencils, with a sheepish look on his face.
Baby said *no* is a very pointy word.
We all took deep breaths and submerged to see what we
Looked like underwater talking about points.
Then you said then what about progress?
Has there been any?
No one really wanted to talk about that, with their hair
All wet.
Baby said there was something moving around in his spaghetti.
He said it made him very happy.

Excavation of the Old Civic Center

Electrical facial expressions,
Frozen hand cushions,
Poison fan blades,
Intoxicated axe-handle beetles on glass shelves,
Plate glass window boxing shadowboxing,
Bonfires, a bonfire of old sounding boards,
Contractual wax knives on a "simple" bib,
Asphalt darning needles, aggregate thread,
Pale green buds, tall tree of brittle pokers,
Leather ribbons, fizz brackets, pistol rockets,
Wafer-thin binoculars, a bee's brain, petals
Of propane, no mention of any rock to crawl
Under, loose fingernails, ribcage hairlock,
Floating water, breathing mechanisms, no
Directions to the entrance to the cave,
No cup, no plate, no three-tined fork,
No important instructions, no milk, no honey,
Not one windowsill to stand a flashlight on,
More than a few spirals, lacerated good
Intentions, a hypothetical heating vent,
Flocks of hair inventories searching for
New homes, some quasi-cattle, strips of rice
Paper fermenting, no warning over the edges,
Jaspered eyes, perpetual re-enactment in
The distance, more than a few expandable
Ladders, crazy teeth, a prophet over to the
Left pulling feathers through a bird's skull,
Somewhere else a baby takes its first step
In an otherwise unconvincing room.

Summertime

The crazy priest threw holy water at the coffin
The way a frycook pops water on his grill to see
If it's fired up or not. But he spoke kindly
Of the man he'd come to bury. He took a long time
Telling the story of how Enoch & God liked to take
Long walks together. He spent a good deal of time
Naming the things they passed and admired, in their
Different ways. Things one wouldn't think Enoch or
God cared a hoot about. Old toasters rusting on
Ditchbanks—why were there so many of them, a book
Swollen with dew—who threw it down, a pocketbook
Turned inside out—had there been a crime, a dogleash
Hanging on a hemlock branch—a clue in a forgotten
Treasurehunt, the left foot of a pair of shoes—
The crazy priest threw holy water at the coffin
As if he were afraid of it. What if a miracle occurred
And the man inside the coffin came back to life?
What if the water were too holy? And when he walked
Around the coffin clattering holy smoke over it
He looked as if he wanted to flee and could not believe
His own eyes. But he spoke well of the man he'd come
To bury. He worked up to the time Enoch & God had
Been enjoying themselves so much they forgot the time
And found themselves closer to where God goes back to
When he leaves here. Now he closed his eyes.
He closed them too long.

Nightshade

As when asked someone says
I'm picturing your blood
Traveling through your fingertips
Up past your wrists.
One sick cookie, I think,
Or just another anybody
Toying with an idea,
Another someone out to scare
Oneself half-to-death,
I'm picturing the air glide
Into your lungs.
I'm seeing smoke explore
The empty spaces there.
Now I'm locking my eyes
And your eyes together
With my astonishingly soulful
Glue and adding on a padlock
And watching it rust and losing
The keys and should we meet up
On Crosspath Road I will say
It was meant to be, look at how
Our ankles look out for one another,
Look at how the nightshade vines
Reticulate in the mountain laurel,
Twisted brother.

Tableaux Vivants

Cracked into with a glass crowbar
You were here
Exposed to mildew, a swarm of bees
You were somewhere else
Triple-exposed & embossed with an inventory tag:
A vague feeling, vaguely nagging, gnawing away
Down in a foundation, below ground
Slaked with feldspar teaspoonsful
Situated around a central whipping post
What did you do when you were there
Organized by degrees of preternatural windsock logic
You disappeared like smoke in a hurricane
Yanked over, pulled through wet sand songs
You leaped down into a bottomless well
Steamed through with on the one hand
You can never get where you're going
You touched a tooth and a tongue, on the other
You can't escape where you've been
In among protective custody, sky, ceiling, skin
Cunning umbrellas, frank helmets & hats
Over there, floor, rug, rug with secret compartments
Woven all through it
You could see what clavicles lead to
A hand pulling a lamb into daylight
A backhoe hard at work in the late afternoon
Workboots, shoelaces, ballet slippers
Where you last stood, what you last said
Nothing on earth was heavy enough
Who touched you then
Waterlines one by one erased by tides
Who would know how to find that now.

Sweet Obsession

It's been eleven days since
I've seen the fox.
Why did you put a whiskbroom
In the suitcase?
From the inside of my face
To the almond-sized bone
Of the soul is a far cry.
Way too wet to hold onto.
I admired how a plain ribbon
Snake shifted into reverse.
Deep in the bottom of my purse
There's a silver knife
With calla lilies carved
On its case. My surface
Remains lily-free for now.
It's been twenty-two days
Since I've seen the fox.
What do you keep in your pocket,
The one where your fingers go
To tell our secrets to subatomic gods?
It's been nine years since
I've seen the fox.
Tiny, tiny, tiny, tiny fox.

When Into the Silence the Silence Gasped

Great big sighs all around. Sigh deeper,
Sigh brighter, sigh fuller, sigh blue,
Sigh pepper, sigh butane lighter, sigh
Theater, sigh carpenter, sigh softshoe,
Sigh yawning vampire, sigh hair on fire,
Sigh particles in suspension, sigh dot,
Sigh sexy circuitry you got there, sigh
Buried cables, sigh screeching raw milk
Cheese, sigh difficult to find brioche,
Sigh ancient handmade miniature steamship
Too dear to take home, sigh rare infinitely
Layered calligraphic tour de force executed
With a pen, sigh that's the saddest pony
I've ever seen, sigh tortured dresses, sigh
The language of divorce, sigh ticket kiosk,
Sigh it's the seventh not the sixth subway
Stop, sigh remember what mother, when we walked
Out the door, said about the milk and cheese,
Sigh, try not to carry the stick like a club,
Sigh, pizzicato, sigh like Augustine did
When he first saw Ambrose reading, sigh like
A princess pulling a fishbone from between
Her lips, sigh like a man finding a seat on
A train, sigh like a far-off wolf singing,
Sigh last lit light switched off,
Sigh parable of the house, sigh yesterday you
Saw a doe what will you see today, sigh fish
Pond, sigh sidewalk, sigh toothpick, sigh ice
Detonation, sigh famished, sigh elaborated,
Sigh approximating, sigh judgment nigh, sigh
Catch-all, sigh what's made such strange bed
Fellows, sigh Sumatran titan arum, sigh it was

Almost imposssible to get a road in edgewise,
Sigh the terrible berry that survives radiation,
Sigh stemcells from micebrains, sigh kerosene,
Rocket, anise, sassafras, chickory & hibiscus,
Sigh not to underestimate the power of worms,
Sigh nanomachines, sigh lice, sigh signified,
Sigh something strong as an ocean dragging
Chainmail over a shoreline, sigh secret hand-
Shake, sigh woodgrain, sigh breastbone, sigh
Nightingale, sigh unanswered prayers, sigh
Unopened letters, sigh address unknown.

Portrait of Me by a Melancholy Man

"I" am seated in his portrait
And "I" am staring at a skull.
I stand for beauty and youth
Which surely will not last
And the skull, well, it stands
For itself and all else that
Will never change. "We" sit near
a table on which rests the biggest
Hourglass "I" have ever seen.
And the three of us, "me," the skull
And the hourglass, have a mirror on our table
To add to our very heavy equation.
A cold mirror, a mirror without eyelids.
"I" think about whose skull I'm eyeing.
"I" wonder who sells skulls and how
Much they cost, and how long good ones
Last. "I" wonder if the hourglass is filled
With salt or sand. "I" look bored to tears,
An inappropriate look, if I do say so myself.
I vividly remember lacking the resources
With which to keep sorrow written all over my
Face. "I" am the least penitent Magdalene,
The poorest contemplative ever to darken
A canvas. I would do it differently today.

Dust

Little misshapen man
Glowing under duskmist,
Pouring over dust, whitepink
Shoulders floating, flanking
A neck outright, adjusted
To the task, two hands, one
Ruffling up dirt, sifting,
The other with a spoon in it,
Now & then, suddenly capturing,
Two quart glass containers,
One for one thing, one for something
Else, working fast on an out-of-the-way
Roadside, furtive, persistent, captive,
Knowing, something so small as to be
Sorted just twice, who is he,
Kneeling in amongst the royal vetch,
Knowing exactly what he wants,
Eternity's thief?

Paradisiac

Colonies of bees colonized our brains.
We could hear them buzzing in and out all day,
Bristling with pollens, loaded with nectar &
Sap. This was good we said, a kind of forti-
Fication. Honeycombs lent a delicate scaffolding
To platforms which otherwise might have been
Crumbling. On a mission, in a hurry, ace restorers
Sorted through everything scarlet, everything blue,
So many shades of green and brown, so many things
Faceted and flashing, hazels, roans and sorrels,
Hectic and fevered, steady and meek, backlog of
Ancient correspondence, bands of dedicated archivists
Traversing vast regions without signposts, back
And forth, without comment, into sublime, into
Ridiculous, without regret, among lost, cunning
And purely blank, from needle to thorn, from wake
Rocking onto shore to a field of fire, from out-
Right lies to words of consolation, from bows &
Arrows to buttons and bows to rags to riches, to
Buckwheat to broomsage to fescue to kumquat to
Avocado and back, and then they were gone.
Into this golden silence we lowered our spoons.

Nine Sunflowers Standing Seven Feet High
Wintering Over in a Snowy Field

My love's mind has made me think
Of the direct path between a sunflower

And the sun, I've watched him be
The only un-sunflower in a field

Of sunflowers in full bloom,
When the hemisphere we happen to be in

Turns to look another way so as to see
More of the fathomless space we oar

And stars, I want to find a place
Where water is, to bring my love with me

There, put down the wooden crates
I carry with me everywhere, and say,

Let's have a seat and stay to watch
The moon come up from underneath the water,

Stars as far beneath the surface as
We can see, a satellite migrating

Among them, we'd follow its path
Directly into one another's souls.

Progress

There was a time when the guillotine meant progress,
Past the hacking axe, the slippery sword,
The gagging hangman's noose.
There was a man who had his head replaced
With a wooden head with one eye on the front
And the other on the westside shaded with a
Green and white striped awning. A little
Windowbox stood under it filled to over-flowing
With sweet-smelling come-give-cream-to-granny
Roses. Purple martins flew in and out of his
Head in the early evening. Little glass lizards
Sunned themselves on him in the morning.
The paperboy really tried to deliver the paper
Very gently. And this, too, was progress.

Shattering of Perfection

You could always tell when
She was about to lose her mind,
She'd begin by stealing flowers
From cemeteries and talking about it
To strangers, by then everyone
Is a stranger, everyone's a friend.
She'd curl into a frond taken away
From spring and she'd stay that way.
She'd drink her wine a thimbleful
At a time and want her meat raw & cold.
A pack of wild kids can steal from the dead
All night long, the dead just laugh at that,
It breaks a blue monotony. But one lonesome
Woman approaching under cover of darkness
Is another matter. There's a jagged logic
As blinding as a seven claw spring trap
To which she's hitched her wagon.
The dead turn away from these flowers.

Nowhere to Hide

Someone writes a name on a slip of paper.
Someone pins it to a wall.
The sun will come up every morning.
Particle by particle the ink will fade
Back into emptiness underneath the paper
Or evaporate and take off into thin air
To ride thermals or reorganize in a thunderstorm
Or the name will have slipped through one of the
Slant cracks there are everywhere in the world.
As the name on the paper disappeared little by
Little, more faint and eventually altogether gone
I was reminded the name had belonged to someone
Who'd always loved the thrill and courage of leaving.
I must have walked by that name on that slip of
Paper ten thousand times.
Little blind thing, stupid eraser.

She Thinks She Hung the Moon

My head is a pincushion for darning needles.
It is an egg containing its brood.
It shares its nest with legions of Roman soldiers.
Perhaps it is over-inhabited.
It does not bite.
My head is a tabernacle, it loves the smell of frankincense.
If my head were a prison it would be empty.
It would be filled with the music of orange blossoms.
My head is a quiver, a patch and a satchel.
It is an arena.
My head is a satellite drifting out of its orbit.
Heads like mine have been found on all seven continents.
They have been linked to life on other planets.
They have been stamped on coins and traded for food.
My head is a nest of boxes, an over-night case.
It has been bombed and looted and sacked.
It has been riddled with scarves, with shoelaces.
My head is an unopened geode, an unopened coconut.
I like to listen to it slosh around.
I like to think of the moon working on it.
My head is a good hiding place, a safe house.
It is where to be in a lightning storm.
It is a cave curtained by a waterfall.

A Walk in Dubuque

On a corner near the edge of town
An empty parking lot, an old hotel,
Nobody in its lobby, no one at the desk,
No one in the hallways, no one under the bed.
Out on the sidewalk heading into the heart
Of downtown, nobody standing in front
Of the empty bank, no one leaning against
A lamppost striking a match on his sole,
No one sprawled on a bench with a newspaper
Over her face. A breeze with no one to touch,
Block after block, nobody, empty, storefront
After storefront, one papered over with dozens
Of signs saying just Be Prepared, some, in
Hiding, with curtains hung on strings. A few
With hand-lettered signs saying Jesus Saves.
No one. No one up ahead stopping to rest
Or walking a dog on a leash. No one.
No one to hear bells start up a long hunt
Into "These Are a Few of My Favorite Things."
No click-click of women's heels, no whoosh
Of a runner's breath, no rattling of change,
As if a plague has visited, as if everyone's
Been abducted, as if the Rapture has really
Happened. No one their hands through
Waterfountains bubbling over. Near the bell-
Tower with no one ringing its bells I turn
Back to look for signs of life. There's a
Horse & carriage coming from far in the distance.
That's when I grab your hand and say, quick,
Run, don't get in.

Need for Secrecy in Secret Societies

Handsignals.
I need to think with you privately.
When the moon looks the other way.
By the stonepath leading to the fountain
After Mr. Blacksheep has shut his cafe
For the evening.
Where Moose hides his bone.
On the front steps of the courthouse
At the entrance to the single-file alleyway.
Inside the shortstop's glove.
Under the cashdrawer in the cash register.
Next to the big pots of citronella.
When bats start up their nightmusic.
Inside the black silk envelope.
On the westbank of the river.
After the bomb stops exploding.
Where the porcupine hides its sewing.
After the field mice have finished with history.
Before the cockroach has taken its throne.
For no more than one lifetime.
When no one else is looking.

Not a Mirror, Not a Keyhole

Down into where nobody knows,
Where if you go there you don't know
How you got there, don't think anymore
You'll be leaving again, meet your new friends,
And you know everything there is to know
About one another, and some say you've come
Through fire, and some have passed through dust,
And some have come through water, and some
By plane, some on horseback, some walked in
Backwards, some talked themselves in, some
Came on skis, some were singing, some coughed
Some came in sleeping and slept and didn't sleep,
Some came with their helmets on, some with forks
In their hands, some jumped, some called it
A big mistake, some had snow on their shoulders,
Some had books in their hands, some whistled,
Some came in chains, some danced, some dreamed,
Some looked surprised, looked relieved, some
Were shivering, some whispered, some came in
Naked and some dressed for church, some crawled,
Some asked to be shown the door, some bellied
Up to the bar, some came with life-jackets on,
Some with bazookas, some in sarongs, some said
It was good to be home, some droned, some came
In dripping wet, some dry as clean bones, some
Had turned into birds, some were bricks, some
Were sticks, some had turned into fish, some
Blushed, some were rats and they stayed rats,
Some cut a wide path, some wore horse-hoof cuffs,
Some talked a blue streak, some had turned into
Old shoes, some said they were experiencing
Deja vu, some said they had something to sell,

Some came prepared, some came without a clue,
Some were honeysuckle, some were rope, some
Smoke, some numbers on a dial, some milk, some
Had turned into saxophones, some had paws,
Some were rivers, some were sheep, some spiders,
Some were threaded needles, some were warm,
Some asked the wind, some asked the fugitive stars.

Two Mules Mulling over the News

Gaunt, knob-kneed
Fool's gold flanked
With smudged black circles around their eyes,
Flop-ears folding & unfolding,
Never in unison,
Pen not an eighth of an acre,
No shelter, dirty water,
Scant straw, no shade,
Racing traffic, shy coyotes,
Stern ravens, razorwire fence,
A certain amount of deep muck,
Damp grain, unshod,
Unturned stones,
Each the other's groom.

Not That Lake

Some lavender blue grayish sort of light lit up
In back of a row of lilacs quick as the lake
A few fingers near a silent switch of the lake
Up higher on a hill eleven or maybe lake
More than eleven tall antennae blinked lake
And unblinked day & night and who would want
To ignore all that said the lake
At first then there were the robber barons who the lake
And there were different kinds of birds by the lake
I could smell smoke of smoking eternally of the lake
I thought all of a sudden that I love the lake
I wanted to go over by the lake
Do you know wheat went out to sea by the lake
Do you know what went on when the lake
You get an inkling and then the lake
You begin to take a drink of water but the lake
You pay out a certain percentage over by the lake
You drift into other worlds and soon enough the lake
Your hand is like the lake
Your hair, the hair on your head, is the lake
I thought lake all of a sudden nearly in the lake
Those trees look weak in the knees for the lake
Gilded icons around the corner are for the lake
Someone's father old in his grave from the lake
Real honest-to-god choir boys singing for the lake
A belted kingfisher made occasional dives into a pond
Near the lake and a yellow-rumped warbler and a pair
Of northern shoveler ducks soon found rest by the lake
What someone thinks someone else remembers by the lake
Anyone will say almost anything to appear to be rational
Next to the lake
It was an exciting week inside the lake

Do you have any plans yet for the lake
Oh, all we needed was just a little bit more of the lake
Friday before last a little before five in the lake.
Quick I'm shot through the heart please call the lake
I now pronounce you man and lake
The girl cut her teeth on the lake
The boy was named after his mother's side of the lake
After so many days of wind and rain the lake came out
And the lake was the way the lake was
And I put my hand on my love's knee under the lake
And my love's head turned and looked into the sea.

Hush

I think the gods were kinder then
When one of us had been harmed or
Torn one of them would look upon us
With pity and turn us into something
New, maybe a catalpa's anther or the
Iridescence inside a wild trout's scale.
Maybe a spider or a nightingale,
A good wrench or a fine lathe,
The headlights of a fast car
Sometimes a god would come along
Who couldn't stand to see us shed
Even one tear. Thus we have endless
Stars. Who gave the undertaker the
Big prize for his parenting advice?

Borderline Case of Insubstantial Vacillating Breakfast Suspense

It's wasn't hard to see lines of direct attachment
strung up between each of the disparate parties
in attendance at the breakfast.
The baby said no hitting.
Invisibility enhanced and deepened their influence.
The baby whispered it's not your turn.
A transparent system of tunnels cluttered the place.
One could see in these all of the variously colored
trails of smoke accompanying feeling and thought.
The baby said crying won't get you anywhere.
One appeared to have become overly detached.
As if one inhabited the place as tenuously as a
recently inducted ghost.
The baby said now what do you say now.
Certainly there were words coming out of their mouths
And inside the words were billions of infinitesimal
bee-like engines of extra-terrestrial origin.
The baby said that's not what you do with spoons.
Everything had at least a dozen hinges on it.
In order for all of the insides to be seen all of the
outsides had been erased.
The baby said no biting.
The technology was still in a fairly primitive state,
The baby said let's zero-in on something.
If one emitted a standard interrogation such as,
"could someone please pass over the aluminum pitcher
of ice cold water without bubbles?" it registered.
The baby said let's triangulate a little longer.
Elsewhere appeared to be exactly where we were, its
latitude and longitude at last assigned, its
population not yet naturalized.

A universal solvent had been released in the area.
There was time to spare, baby said.
One at a time we disappear.

No Substitute

While you were gone
I spent some time at your big oak table
With your lanky tulips & brassy amaryllis.
They say things about you that would burn
Your ears. Fair to say, they worship you
And one can do worse than be worshipped
By pistil and stigma and anther and style.
Their tribute kept me company so long there
In the long night, with its twin flames
And big wine glass and white-washed frog
On an errand from a god and a moose with
A broken antler. They talked about you
As if you were here and wanted to amuse
You with their petally gossip & laughter
In their pollenish way. The fork you left
On your plate couldn't be mistaken for a
Hand fallen asleep, not by amaryllis and
Tulips. Being flowers, they're never
That desperate, so near despair. Don't
Worry, none of us talked about where you
Were or why you'd gone, we made plans
For what we'd do when you returned.
And you were never gone.

A Split Second

We picked up the handset of a telephone, someone
Whispered us a question about what sort of faith
We put in popular elections, we said things
That instantly crossed one another out, we moved
As one to sit on a chair by a kitchen window,
We paused to pick up a glass of water, one of us
Wanted to remember so many things over and over
And one of us said that's done with, one of us
Had a grandfather who'd never read a book, another
Led a reform party and wrote seven manifestoes,
There were brown paper bags filled with seeds,
Animals to butcher and animals to husband & tame,
Birds in wooden cages on ropes in persimmon trees,
A beat-up truck with dirt on its windshield,
A rifle to break down and clean, there were cuff
Links to thread through cuff link holes in starched
White shirts, bones everywhere, fingerprints
Deactivated, one of us wanted to picture hearts
Beating all over the world, to think about what hands
Do, in general, what ears have in common, what feet
Are usually for, how eyes seem to epitomize optional
Points of view, one of us has a friend who likes
To spend a certain amount of time in sensory depri-
Vation in her imagination she's a human sacrifice
In a religion no one practices any longer, she's
Strapped on a log moving opposite the speed of light
In a dark tunnel on a conveyor belt with the scent
Of hot sawdust and sparks of splintering metal
To keep her company, we get up from our chair,
Chills graze along our antennae, we hold onto our glass
Of water, we close our eyes, I carefully put your
Head back where it belongs.

Translated from the Danish

My soul wants a mouse, baby, yes
I am cranked. Palm trees shiver
My disco smash blast haiku haiku.
Get in with me into swimming pools,
Go with me down to the terror shores,
Bathe terribly in every sort of quartz
Bowl. But do not open the shoeshine
Boxes. Them boxes turn bad as touching
Tabernacles. Stay away from mosaics
And don't babysit the pheasants anymore.
Enough of that victim with me stickiness.
I like a good strong stick and stiff eye-
Lashes, I like southern California very
Much. I osmosis most quickly in a closet,
Excellent toggle, excellent rotary blade,
Excellent eye examinations, excellent tender
Horseshoes. I am not in love with my psy-
Chiatrix. No, I am not, not at, not even,
Not something, some place in America,
And then some mouse I'd wanted to help
My soul along grew the horns of an ox,
Some mouse. I want to thank you all for
Being with us this evening in Emily Dickinson.
We are the first Danes to land here.
We will save you from her terrible baby shoes.

Gegenschein

Someone has over-stimulated the celestial animals
It takes a trillium
Ditto for turtles
As when an oven dislikes a sink
Somewhere in the vicinity is human eyeliner
It feels something like bartering
Too much had been attached to a coat check
Rustled, looted, laid aside
Appearing in part 2 are saber-toothed tiger teeth
And in several places custom-made musical instrument cases
Blazing near Los Alamos
Every last bit of the cuneiform has been plagiarized
Inside every astronomer stands a rapt emerald shepherd
A segment remained without a picture of water or a waterfall
Somebody said somebody said all secrets have been counted
They set out for the land of 14,474
After auspicating with abandon
They slept in the North Frame
At last an aurora borealis realized above Yellowknife
Blue zinnias unfurled
Soon bartering began in earnest
Some success with tincture of arnica
A secret campaign had been waged against coyotes
Rabbits covered everything in sight
Scarlet ones with razor blades for eyes
Groove faster into counterglow

Proof of the Fire

A true believer puts his finger on it
And turns his back on everything else.
A skeptic turns his back to it
And warms his hands on windowglass.
Monks agree to sing and pray
And rotate their eyeballs north of trespass.
A merchant knows a good thing when he sees it
And figures on his fingers how to make it scarce.
The lord of the fire points to a blind man
And the blind man has never seen his own face.
The blind man's face is wet.
He thinks it's been licked by the dog of water.
Dried out by hands of the wind.
Slathered by wolves of regret.

A Bird I've Never Seen

They yellowed everywhere.
We saw them yellow for anything.
They sulphured before it all.
I saw and nothing comes of it none too soon.
Some wood is small, too small to saw.
Sometimes too many children, too many collarbones.
I saw the back of my left hand into delicious matchsticks.
I make a mess of matchsticks.
I saw up a mess of everything and it tastes all right.
It might kill me tomorrow.
I saw a mighty oak.
I saw someone eating, really eating, and liked it.
I saw someone climb, climb slowly, into a bed.
I saw myself in half and then some.
I saw seven ways out of everything far away from me.
I can't say I saw more than I saw without knowing it,
Without looking in, without drowning in it.
I saw something at the bottom of it all.
I saw a point floating as far as an eye can see.
Crybaby at the crack of dawn, peacock snatcher.
I saw a long way around straight through the middle
Where the edges meet.
I saw a chair with no one sitting on it.
I saw its slats and its spindles and its spine.
I saw all morning through a thin whistle.
I saw as if my life depended on it.
I saw through the middle of one unbroken night.
I saw through the pauses in a sad friend's voice.
I saw through the creases in a dead friend's scarf.
I saw as if the sun went down in the water twice.
I saw because you won't let go of my hand.
I saw my pointless inching through a purple copse.

Romantic

My love said take
All my books,

You can take all my clothes,
My hats, my shoes, my gloves,

You can have my watchband
Take my sifters

You can have my glass head
And my silver darts,

Take my wild boar, my astronaut,
You can have my pots & pans,

And my replica
Of the United States, and take

While you're at it, all of the
presidential figurines

You can have all my matchbooks,
My binoculars, my exceptionally fine

Collection of cleaning products,
My one-of-a-kind snake charming horn,

Take my sand dollars & beach glass,
Take all of my spices and salt & pepper,

You can have my smoked ham & brown mustard,
You can take away my Progresso Soup,

Take away my bread, take my spoons,
You can have my sheets and my pillows,

Take my rugs and my three erasers,
Take my pitcher and the scarf you gave me,

Take my feathers my fox took
From my hawk, take my walking stick,

You can have my broom and my glass eye,
You can take away my atomic clock,

Take my dog, take my rule book,
Take my decoy and my bamboo cage,

You can take my girl waiting on
Her suitcase, my Michael Jackson doll,

You can take my mother and her priest
And their holy water basin,

Take my drill and my hammer,
You can have all my brushes & combs,

Take my handkerchiefs and my scissors,
Take all of the keys you can find

In the house, take my scythe my hoe,
My rags, my lamp with the lovers

Asleep in one another's arms, take
My sprite sitting on a stump daydreaming

Over an empty book, take my moose,
Take my coffee can of loose change,

Take all of my ant traps, take my
Windowpanes, take my steps and my doors,

Take my chicken shack & my wheelbarrow,
Take my combat ship plaque, take my

Vatican champagne flutes, my earplugs,
Take my quilts, take all of my quilts,

I would not take one stitch
Of one of your quilts, though I love them,

I sweetly interrupted.

Edges in Creases

There went a wisp wasp on a leash with whiplash.
Everything in the backlash bank lacked rouge.
We'd take care of everything in the morning.
It is morning, isn't it morning, it's morning.
Thank you very much. Such as it is, red.
I wish there were more flambeaux everywhere.
It was better before the tuxedos exploded.
Twang, as in let fly love's pierciful arrows.
If it was tusks they wanted tusks it would be.
Swanking along without underbrush overhead.
Their beat, their dust, their sorry eyes.
You could see how deeply inspirational exhaustion
Bored some of them things, what are they called?
Lock of hair? Blue jar of gallstones? Stalemate?
There were nine glasses of milk lined up along.
I stayed inside a paperweight a fortnight.
I came out quarterly but lived too far away.
Feathers were flying. They discussed repaving
Their faces. My pajamas were sleeping
With one another in someone else's dreams.
Liars are more gullible than infants.
Liars are swimming gorgeous underwater.
Twice in one letter he wrote it was as if
A suicide found the water too cold.
He also said he saw the reaper below
Between the iron bars of his cell.
He said there was more than enough room
In an asylum, he said what a queer thing
The touch is, the stroke of a brush.
He went looking to find who'd cut down
His fence. He was very proud of his sheep.

A Walk Up the Even and Down the Odd Sides of a Street

A door you can get into a house through opens,
Down go your satchels & baskets & bushels,
A leaf's on the edge of a rug,
Bit by bit a staircase begins to make sense,
I had been looking too long into strangers' eyes
And I would make a note to stop doing that,
Some other time I could gaze, I could listen,
What's in your coat pocket tonight,
Were you thinking love's a demon reasoning,
How many ways were there for being around a table,
It hurts to watch words say things no one knows,
You went to sleep last night, most likely,
I did for a while,
I like it in there when something you want to keep
Follows you out,
A girl made two mistakes and she liked them both,
There was live ammunition in their heirlooms,
I saw a dozen owls in the space of two moons,
But they whoo-ed not for me more than twice,
For a while I adhered to a mailbox, a collection
Plate slid down the aisle, columns of numbers
Had been penciled in the margins, I was allowed
To put up a white flag so the country doctor
Could come and find us,
He boiled his needles in a little enamel pot,
He wiped steam from his eyeglasses with a corner
Of the tail of his dirty white shirt.

Cord of Wood, Spark of Shoes

For a while in back of stepped aside in case not even close
Still wanted a better view and this worked for a while until
Something someone said changed the terms in favor of after all
This time and all of a sudden wanted to start over with as soon
As possible after almost out of sight returned with someone
Thought better of it almost too late to make much difference
And for a while nothing went on but some sighs and a couple of
Gasps now and then found in an out of the way place second
Thoughts were having profound effects in the first place or
At least after too close to call backed off without how could
It be to begin with and found something someone touched under
Somehow something must have mattered slowly returning almost
As if nothing had happened and as if nothing else at least
For the time being could possibly be more important than that
And is so everything would have to be might come around more
And more often and forever might reverse itself at last time
This happened it wasn't what anyone thought it was really wanted
It to be not that that mattered so much and would for a while.

Poem for Another Poem

When I looked away you were gone.
I saw your constellation of pitch, light,
Scale, nuance and addition, as fine as the
Edge of a leaf, as sufficient as ice, as
Insistent. You stood in my line of sight,
So still you were there, it shifted as if
A god's hand had lent itself to mine. You
Moved in ways brains move to work their ways
Through crowds or long halls randomly lit.
You showed me a bronze shield under a morning
Star. You showed me cunning. You came close
To me. You went away. There was nothing
In the universe that didn't surround you.
You were thinner than a blade of winter grass.
I saw how you took a broken twig for granted,
As if it were your sister or your brother,
How you were almost nothing. You zigzagged
Over fine dirt, a fingernail, a scratch in
Sifted sand. Then a wave dragged desire
Back into green water. A thread found its
Way through air, a thread no one had knotted.
Then you stopped. You were what stopped.
And you were hidden. You weren't hiding.
I think you were thinking about March 27th.
Which century? Nobody else in the world.

Separate Worlds

Girl working her footsteps down into snowcrust,
Flat black back dissolving in snowmist & fog,

Now comes her brother walking behind her, walking
Sweetly, directly in her footsteps, as if he were

Being careful not to disturb her, as if she might
Be one thing all to herself, on her own workshift,

And he didn't want to change anything, nothing at
All. He had something big to say, said it,

Said it, and had nothing more to say, he found
Some stairs, a fire and a funny story, he found

Some sheep, a sleeping donkey & some funky angels
Sleeping in a pasture, he found a splinter,

Found a note he'd been looking for, found more
Room somewhere there was no room before, found

A short yellow pencil with toothmarks in it,
Some dirt on the knees of his jeans, found

Himself waiting and waiting and he found that
Fine by him, no where to go, to have to be,

And afterwards he found himself at home,
And soon enough he put on his coat to leave again,

He walked through a cloud to get to where his sister
Was, she was breaking a stick of chalk into small

Bitesize pieces, his mouth was dry, her eyes were bronze
Tablets into which fabulous secrets had been burned.

Assorted Angels Comforting the Damned:
a ransom note

Everywhere there's nothing but atmosphere,
It lifts away like an eggshell away from an egg,
And there inside a neverbefore breathed air
A stick breaks open, a stone cricket creeps out,
Getting ready to sing, better leave it be.
Another cool customer comes in for a landing,
A tall thin man with a snake draped around
His neck "to keep him cool." Better leave
That one alone. I am standing on a shoreline,
blue water, black stones, not much to go on.
No, I am sitting in a red chair with ropes
Around my ankles & my wrists. I've heard trains
Go by, heard a chainsaw start up, heard a kid's
Voice commanding his troops to be brave, to hang
Tough. I was carried on the back of a horse,
I was stowed in the hull of a boat. A hand
That smelled of cinnamon and tobacco smoke opened
My mouth. My feet fit into footprints on the floor,
Something creaked, someone sneezed, somewhere
Something slammed a door.

Translation Work

The leaves blew around and spun and knocked
Into one another rushing back up into the trees
To re-attach themselves to their twigs.
They grew green after they'd been brown and
Dishwater gray and red and orange and yellow.
They began to grow smaller, shrinking and curling
A little and eventually they went back inside
Their buds and took deep breaths and sucked
Themselves back into stems and limbs and deep
Down into trunks and they looked all around
Themselves in disbelief and said, oh my, look
At us we are headed straight down into the earth.

Good Detective

Then find out who picked apart the Badlands
And made them beautiful.
What do you want to know about armbands?
Tell me something to do with time.
Who picked out blue, who coiled smoke?
Make a list of anything you've ever thrown
Into a river, peachpit, bones, broken mirror,
Wedding band, telephone, tape recorder, nails,
Staple gun, empty cans, a heavy suitcase, a
Worn out hammer, etc., something you wrote
And sealed inside a bottle, something you
Couldn't say to anyone else. Who signed
Your birth certificate? Were you born
A dust storm, do you remember the doctor's
Hands. Who said a little too much is enough
For me? Make a list of anything
More than two of. Make a list of nothing
You've ever borrowed. Who wound rope?
Find out where the pocketknife went.
Find out why the hunter put an elk's head
In the blackoak. Who picked out livid violet?
Find out who owns everyone's water rights.
What happened around the blue baize table?
Who donned a dusty apron and dirty cotton shirt?
Who made a mundane glory in the precincts of the
Arena? Find out why if magnetic resonance
Imaging changes quantum states patients emerge
Seemingly unchanged. When will the path past
The churchyard be filled with cherry blossoms?
What's behind the green door? What's with the
Hysterical fugues? Why is mad-traveling the
Most "natural" way to be insane? Find out who

Was creeping around "mental hygiene." Why
Was a customer afraid to leave the pharmacy?
Find out a way to be invisible.
Not like a ghost, find a way around that.

What In Heaven Is That Little Inlaid Box Doing?

What's the butterfly on the blind girl's shawl up to?
Are there too many shawls in the cornfields?
I ran into a sentence with *intensity, lushness, elegance,*
Gorgeousness and *freshness* in it.
It was a sentence about understatement & balance.
In a chapter about fragrance.
In a paragraph about being careful to scent one's self
With things that might attract the right sort of attention.
It came with a warning to mind the difference between
    reflection
And refraction. Out came our manuals of optics and physics.
We rested our eyes on some two-fisted orchids.
One of our many weaknesses were oysters.
There was a plain brown farmcat in the foreground.
Why did it look as if he had no lungs?
Who put wine-stained corks where their noses used to be?
There was a pale woman with a paler scroll
Standing inside his head, waiting for a train,
A train everyone could see was not going to come.
I felt sorry for a boy who said he gagged on his first communion.
I dreaded his sense of doom.
It's not pretty when a kid's hero gets cut down to size.
Once I hid for nine hours in a haystack.
I felt a burning desire to be inside an aquarium.
I felt a burning desire to be embroidered on a shawl.
We followed the footprints til we came to the end of the stubble.
A burning needle, a moss-covered field in bloom,
A river nobody's walked on or crossed, what lightning did
To the fragrance of rain.
It was all right to walk on the traintracks.
Light went down to the bottom of the lake.
They covered the mirrors with what they could find.

Many of them felt tenderly toward their genitals.
The scarf was delivered in a plain brown wrapper.
The sketch was just a sketch.
There was still 2,000 miles to go.
The engineer's son lost his finger in the brake case.
He was so afraid it was going to touch his teeth.
He'd sentenced himself with no hope for parole.
I'd never been around so much nostalgia.
I ran away when they set it on fire.

How Ghosts Housesit

An empty house is cold
As it should be when you are away
As it should when you are gone
Its chilly hallway fumes with mold
Nothing much moves near some roses
Though they last longer in a cold room
Than they would if you were home
A bed of ashes where you banked a fire
A penny on a rug a pushpin on a sill
A blue thread caught over a black doorlatch
Water in a bowl on the floor
At night all of the beds sleep alone
As they should when you are gone
No one pulls the curtains closed
A spoon stays in a cup you left
At the top of a staircase
No one wears your clothes
A light you left on in a closet keeps burning
As it should when you've gone away
A note leaning against a stack of stamped
Envelopes no one reads
A bowl of pears & papaya ripens more slowly
Than it would if you were home
A key stays where you left it in its lock
As it should when you are gone
Edges of a photograph of the inside of a mouth
Curl, there may be a little more rust blossoming
On several crooked mirrors when you return

Rich Sense of Uncertainty Troubled by Indeterminacy

Leaning a little in, slant-prone toward
A simple view, we considered their mutable eyelids .
And then they opened their eyes
And then we dissolved
They looked for us where we never were
Some nights we preferred two moons
And the moon went along
Once they took us straight away to sit on a lonesome bench
Where no sooner did we sit we saw a blurry fox cross
A crooked path between lines of feeble powerlines
And no sooner did we see it, they motioned
It was time to take us back and we went off in all directions all
At once all the while rocking back and forth between the next
Appointment we might keep and the apparently successful
Completion of our chance encounter they referred to as
Appointment with virtually unverifiable evidence.
We felt like foxes with our heads cut off.
Maybe it had something to do with all the faux fata morgana
We'd tried to hide in their chimney, there was too much smoke
In the gravy, we'd spied too long on the figments.
For desultory reasons too capricious to go into we could often
Be found in the vicinity of a stump on which a puzzled chicken's
Bewildered head had just been decisively cut off and we could
Often be seen dazed not knowing what to make of all the errant
Blood we came to be spattered with while the two parts of what
Had been one hen looked as if they would do anything to find
One another again and when they did it would be as if nothing
Had happened at least that's what they said as they opened the
Pneumatic doors of an enigmatically nonplussed aluminum bus
And beckoned us on to go wherever next which way they wanted.
Sometimes they took us to the place loons loomed over us

And we would do everything we could to stay there
But they wouldn't let us
Some nights we were lucky to have just one moon
And on these nights they tucked us into our random beds
As if something like the sun might come up in the morning.

Wagonload of Freshly Sprung Potatoes

Region went that a way, the this, and what
About last night leaning against thirsty stars,

Moon out of control, landing and unlanding
Over destabilizing hills. It used to be a town,

Now it's a laboratory and it looks bad for mice.
Am I a mouse, sweet little babies of every sex say,

Am I going to Heaven? What should we take to the
Grave? There were no more cars, no one wanted to

Drive cars anymore, no body felt safe in any car
Seat, front or back, strapped in by a belt, afloat

On what were called ferry boats, even in petri dishes.
Big petri dishes, bigger by far than any ever before.

I wish I were spiral bound. Even if it's written on
Water there's a good chance it can still be revised,

If the noon and the stars are still listening, if the
Hydrometer isn't entertaining a gag order. The

Concocted chiefs of the laboratory told us in so many
Words we could not believe our eyes we would be altered

A little, not so much that we'd know we noticed, you
Understand, but enough, enough by a very long shot.

Burr, it was weird inside our burnooses in those days.
This way to the hot tank, keep off the bunsen burners,

No spirit writing at this time, time to take a culture,
Lights out anytime, lose the long faces, this is the

Laboratory, it is within these walls dense enough to
Stop a tank you will be done, you may be terrorbred,

It left us kind of flabbergasted, sort of out of sorts
Though just as curious as ever. Stunned to be applied

Such as fingernail paint might be applied to an
Acrylic thumbnail. Yes, your thumbscrews are to be

Admired, never has anyone ever gazed upon more
Quintessential thumbscrews. It was so much better

Out there in the spiral galaxy where wagonloads
Of potatoes, muddy, crusted with mud, lumbered

Thoughtfully toward the distillery. The slides
Were always as cold as ice as cold as the dark

Side of the moon. We hadn't been afraid of barrettes
Until now. I had never been stapled before.

I'd had several titanium screws drilled in my skull
A long time ago. But then that was necessary.

I have a cousin who spent ten years in prison for doing
Something no one deserves to do to someone who deserved

Better than that. Today he's captain of a ferryboat.
Potatoes have a reputation for saving at least one nation.

And they have eyes. And like worms they can be cut into
Many pieces and spontaneously combust. They can be

Distilled into a fuel more or less efficient enough
To burn inside internal combustion engines. Same can

Be said for moguls. Barons of petroleum products,
Of laboratory-grade ore, captains of this, stewards of

That, our time spent with you has been more fun than
A barrel of monkeys. Not real monkeys.

Grief Comes & Goes As It Pleases

No one tonight under boiling stars,
Inside zeroes. Just part of a hand
Left, half-erased, all sidewise.
Like a bird with its ear to the ground,
Pausing, listening for the high whine
Dirt gives off as it moves through worms.
Part of a curse, part of a cure.
I'd looked forward to your asking
So many difficult things.
How do you know they're fish?
How can you tell it's a swallow?
What makes you so sure it's a moose,
How do you know when to kiss,
What's all the crying about,
Which way does the wind blow
To tell a hawk from a handsaw,
What passes through a screendoor,
A cup of milk & a black leather wallet,
What's lashed to heartvalves & kneecaps,
To rhizomes and a bucket of ashes,
What's the last thing you touched,
What part of a face do you like,
What part of your story do you say
Over and over, how can you tell it's
A step ladder, how do you know it's a
Boat on a lake, why do you still want
Your coat, where, if you could go
Anywhere in the world, would you go,
What, if you could be any bird in the
World, would you be, how do you see
With your eyes closed, what do you see
With your eyes closed, how can you tell
That they're closed. What do you want
With us, worms, noisy dust.

Weak Little Title Ashamed to Be So Exposed

Timid little title abashed to be so highlighted
Massive brute of a body of lines dominating a
Pathetic little title for no cause, cruel brute
Bullying a shy little title over nothing, some
People, finding quarrels everywhere, ex-zones.

Tame Swans

The gristmill's gone
Though the river isn't

An oak's been quartered and drawn
And carted to town and stacked

In two cords on the edge of a lawn
There were eggs in the air

Most of them didn't break
There was a suitcase patched

In three places with black ducttape
Waiting at the bottom of a staircase

When it's cold outside it's not a good idea
To be inside standing by a window breathing on it

A message arrived as a rocketship flies
There was a menacing kindness in the eyes of a stranger

A note of alarm in the voice of a neighbor
A nuthatch looking at itself in an invisible mirror

Every other house was empty
Every other house had someone living in it

The flags were all gone
But the wind wasn't

For a while no one missed leaves
For a long time everything was a blur.

A Tango We Negotiated to Turn Our Train Around

Irony is about killing your father, blinding
Yourself, and sleeping with your mother, not
Necessarily in that order. It haunts the ice
Cone a wise-eyed baby licks in the zoo house
While it watches a gorilla suck on a tick it's
Just pulled from its neck. A periscope is one
Of the funniest sights in the world and one of
The most un-ironic. A periscope would not know
Irony if it came up and bit its nose off. Radar
Isn't ironic either, but for different reasons.
There's something about having a personal rela-
Tionship with God that seems sort of ironic but
Perhaps isn't. In the year 2000 there were 2000
Tigers in the U. S. state of Texas. A travesty,
Most likely, though not ironically. An American
Couple deciding to marry on Bora Bora in a tra-
Ditional Tahitian ceremony should involve some
Kind of irony but apparently didn't. The thrill
With which the young man from Prague whipped
Potatoes was catching and definitely not ironic.
Sometimes someone's forehead will seem to have
Scars on it where its antlers have been removed.
Sometimes a scar is all there is.

The Cold War

I suppose I wanted an icepick.
Or it wanted me and who am I late in the afternoon
could have fooled an assembly of interrogators.
A fawn had walked across the lawn.
I'd been chilled to the bone.
One of them said we could do without spoons.
One threw rocks and one threw stones.
One took the money and ran.
One had a pail and one had a bucket.
Suppose what we did was maim the Holy Grail?
On purpose, by accident to keep an even keel.
I don't think the moon plays favorites.
I don't think we resemble bees.
Suppose we had to do without roses.
What's the difference that it really happened?
I did what I was told and stayed with the horses.
We lived together on a floating island.
Do you remember what happened with the floating baby?
Do you remember what we hid and why it was hidden?
Does it matter what could never be found?
If we'd found it would we have put it in practice?
One of them trained an oak to grow up a lattice.
I'm in awe of involuntary muscles.
Is there anything better than photosynthesis?
I did what I was told and slept with the fish.
We lived together in a cold cracked place.
Do you remember where you hid a block of hot ice?
Do you remember what the blankets were for?
A dog disappeared in a basket of fog.
I don't think we resemble dogs.
I hid inside a footprint and did what I was told.
Nothing didn't really happen I suppose.

Hat On a Pond

Fish dragging banners behind them,
Expeditions to higher elevations,
Herd of white deer, half a red pear,
Throat of fingerdeep black fur,
Octagonal amber ashtray with a
Handful of bullets in it, sweeping
Up wooddust, sweeping up and down
Not against the grain, pitchers of
Icecold water, pitchers of gravel &
Sand, spine flickers, throat catchers,
Breaking string of black pearls,
Eyes in search of eyelids, handprint
On thin air, footprints on thresholds,
Look out for falling cooks, make way
For Miss Thornbird, leaf loose on
Windowledge, black cat with white eye-
Mask, anyone with knowledge of, awestruck
Matchstick, scarlet blouse loose on
Fire escape, fish explaining to a hat
What it will do with the rest of its life.
Hat close, getting there.

This Drug Is Wanted Bitter Bad, Sir, Whatever For

Dead of noon, weird birds, little room
To breathe, electric skin resectioning
Charges firing, near fission, clairvoyance
Contraption rattling, God's pseudonyms
Scrolling over dirt roads, oak alias elm
Alias otter alias wall of water alias
Coin alias cork alias corona alias key
Alias cloud alias azure alias faithful
Leaf-cutting bee alias progressive beefly
Alias legionary ant alias bittersweet
Alias dock alias thorn alias chair alias fence
Alias tooth alias blade alias brake alias
Wrench alias shutter release alias bench
Alias hind paw alias fingernail alias
Landing gear alias badge number alias
Headband alias dingbat alias rotary
Alias umbrella alias matchflare alias
Soul alias ribs alias living wage alias
Toehold alias sound barrier alias tender
Spot alias tent alias boat alias parade
Alias lily alias porch alias cave alias
Tentacle alias thumb alias grip alias
Mouse alias feather alias scale alias
Bridge alias membrane alias mirror alias
Moon alias chromosome alias wind alias
Timezone alias ferry alias tunnel alias
Soup alias bread alias thistle alias fig
Alias window ledge alias grape alias
Towtruck alias whistle alias alibi,
Dead of noon, weird birds.

Idiographic

Lawns scattered with ghosts, with clothes on,
Ghosts who shouldn't be waving wave anyway
And their arms fall off. They float away.
Ghosts with party hats, with tape measures.
One with a shovel looking for a grave digger,
One with a funnel looking for a little to add
To a lot, one with a pocket full of quarters
With a soft spot for parking meters, one with
An unforgettable story about an exuberant dachs-
Hund, one with a cursed dowry, with a whimsical
Yet profound look at atomic medicine, one with
Outstanding genealogy, one with answered prayers,
One on a jag analyzing recent political peccadilloes
In light of biblical prophesy, eye-opening & disturbing,
That one, one with a full set of teeth looking for an
Open mouth, one with a branding iron in search of a
Soulmate, one with a skeleton key looking for an unlocked
House, one with an axe looking for a block of ice, one
With a can of gasoline and a box of kitchen matches, one
With a mallet looking for a wicket, one with a dozen eggs
Looking for a hen house, one with milk looking for a milk-
Ing barn, one with a cup of water looking for a river,
One with a dictionary searching for a library, one with
Loops of rope looking for a field of hemp, one with a
Searchlight, one with a wounded snake, one with a vat of
Permanent white dye, one with a sweat, one with a nose-
Bleed, one short of breath, one with a hairbrush, one with
A comb, one with a full head of hair, one with a foghorn,
One with perfume on, one walking through a town banging a
Bone on the sweet side of a snaredrum.

Search

Make an unconscious decision to uncover a wall
(maybe there will be priceless tracing or graffiti
with a message in its signs warning you away from
reading anything into it or interpreting anything
personally (I'm thinking of languages I can speak
without understanding a word of what I'm saying (
of words that go around not knowing what they mean)
(of that excellent question if salt has lost its
saltness wherefore with what will you season it)

Or a packet of parchment tied with raffia, nine
or so pages (their edges ragged as if torn by hand
or hand-made that way with fibers & feathers &
lint & hair & shredded pieces of other pages) dusted
with streaks of wood shavings, spotted and foxed,
a little creased (I'm thinking of pages one knows
someone's hidden (and of why we sometimes hide
something we want to hide in such a way so that
some time later a long time after it will be uncovered;

Or discovered or re-discovered if it hasn't disintegrated
or burned or been shredded or dissolved) (of who
someone's pictured, it couldn't be anyone someone couldn't
imagine, a long way off in the future, no, it can't be
anyone anyone knows (its intention would correspond
to that of a message in a bottle rather than one in a
capsule tied to a homing pigeon's red, wrinkled leg)
(nor can it be likened to that of an envelope stamped
with someone's special pleading *not to be opened until*

A gasoline flare attached to a bamboo cane
bloodhounds miserable longings through fog
on all four sides we were surrounded by water

a steady line of icebergs fell over the horizon
when the waves stopped coming we changed our thinking
an airliner & all of its passengers entered into a cloud
it was almost impossible to get them out of their baths
we could find vernal pools by looking for patches of fog
every night we fell asleep a little too close to the fire

(I'm thinking of north, south, east, west as sides
of something (I can cross myself without thinking)
instead of corners and curves and curtains & caves
(we counted we had eleven scissors but no pinking shears)
& if we were surrounded, encircled, something would
have to be explained via pie chart in order for us to
do something in some kind of arbitrary proportion
to what the essential formal simplicity (it wouldn't
be elegance or ferocity) begs to be brought to bear)

This time when they said, *we feel bad but we don't
know why*, we took them at their word
and we held their hands and we stroked their brows
and we let them rest their heads in our laps
and we rocked them back & forth & side to side
and we sang them old lullabies (and stopped
that when they sobbed for us to not)
and we never asked them why or why not,
and we never asked them to explain themselves

So this was what distilled in the whispering
gallery, *thousands of scarlet ibis roasting
on a desk* (it should have been roosting at dusk)
*slivers of secret biscuits, only the best race
horses* (100,000 DNA samples from some of the wild
Spanish horses) (mixed feelings in the presence
of gardenias) *everyone of them escaped their families*
(no!) *we hummed them old alibis* (we worked in the
dirt) *we counted eleven thousand knots in a net*

When we went back to look a hand on a latch was
the only thing left (you could tell what time it was
by whether or not there were bomb shelters or which
way a train aimed or who had what on or what animals
were doing or if there were shadows or how many voices
(I'm thinking of voice recognition devices, facsimile,
ventriloquism, impersonation (to ridicule or to mock
or to fool), simulations, counterfeits and mimics)
and how they sounded because of what they were saying)

Camouflage in the cloisters, camouflage in court,
an ever-present set of circumstances into which one
can pretend to blend in or stand out from depending
on what's at hand in the buckets of paint, feathers
& scales, great swaths of titanium sheaths, little
pots of rouge & smoking blue tints department and
who's around with an eye for seeing what's so much
there it can be called upon to help us disappear
if to do so buys a little time which is part of a plan

(*Plans change* has that sound of some kind of
sickening disappointment embedded in it, I guess,
unless you're the one delivering it, and even then
you might not like it that what you thought you wanted
you didn't or what you planned couldn't afterall (it
makes me think of reasoning and to what ends it appears
anyone might go to sound rational and within reason
many rational means have their characteristic twists
& turns & are as useful as a key is if it fits a lock)

(That's not strictly true (a full pound iron skeleton
key hanging on a nail has to my knowledge no lock not
anywhere near here and a ring of old master keys lying
on a table in a hall is nothing more than a random
collection I couldn't throw away (it's practically
impossible to discard something as suggestively
simple as a key (and most of them are small enough)

and if it were where (would all of them need to be
ceremoniously carried down to the banks of a river

You can lie down on it and have someone trace your
outline, you can dampen it with seaweed and wrap
a fish in it, you can layout seeds on it to dry, you
can use it to line the bottom of a cage, you can
make a kite out of it, you can use it to swat a fly,
you can stop a hole in a torn out screen with some,
you can find pictures in it to give to a child to
color over, you can fold it the way a paper accordion
flag (no not flag fan) is folded for starting a fire

Eventually almost everyone is packing and unpacking
a few boxes or throwing something into a suitcase
or moving methodically through all of the pockets
on a backpack evidently finding some things entirely
forgotten (a wrinkled notebook with its spiral spine
crushed, a thumbnail size totem of a rabbit (scratching
an ear) made of plastic, a braided bracelet in volatile
colors, a polaroid snapshot of a forest of t.v. antenna
over San Luis Potosi) & other things a little at a time

Far, far away, so far it's impossible to get there
(and it may turn out not to be anywhere a line, a laser,
a length of rope or anything for that matter anything
can seek to find (someone's recently walked by the foot
of a bed, humming something loving, pausing to make
note of something) (rising & falling like mercury in
a thermometer) (transphysical, ultracollateral, fix-
ating) (a moonraking for some faraways with out of reach
its very soul, jumping off place in the middle of nowhere)

My love looked at me as if I'd just asked how far is the
east from the west (we were face to face) without saying
why this question should be up for discussion at this

time afterall everything related must have been settled
eons ago and weren't there more pressing questions we
could go right up to the water's edge and then swerve
& slow down & stay by the water until the cows come home
is how they keep you to themselves to be alone

(Not so fast) In case after case so urgent was
it has now become clear the difficulty remains
in fact the trouble with there is also here is
(ergot-o-mania in the ice house, never enough
equity of redemption, listening to them break
someone down (nothing you wouldn't be comfort-
able with) with bait too disgusting to describe,
so there it is, the irreparable harm, a swarm
as in the beach swarms with children summer evenings

A stream of water flew down a trough in a banister,
serpentine walls had a good idea what they were
doing with shade, what wind wanted wind could have,
oleander & bougainvillea & aloe vera (as big as
the head of an elephant (there can be elephants
walking wherever they want) long since that won't
begin, without any warning, a long while ago going
away unexpectedly into a preglacial dawn,
atavistic, unwritten, some fine day, hence on the brink of

About the Author

Dara Wier is the author of eight books of poetry. Grants from the Guggenheim Foundation, the National Endowment for the Arts, and the Massachusetts Cultural Council have supported her work. In 2001, she was awarded the Jerome J. Shestack Prize from *American Poetry Review*. She teaches at the University of Massachusetts in Amherst.

About the Book

Cover drawing by Guy Pettit.
Cover design by J. Johnson.
Book design by Brian Henry.
Set in Minion.
Printed on acid-free, recycled paper by Thomson-Shore.